THE

VAGINA

MONOLOGUES

Eve Ensler

VILLARD

NEW YORK

Originally produced by HOME for Contemporary Theatre and Art
at HERE, Randy Rollison, artistic director, and Barbara Busackino,
producing director, in association with Wendy Evans Joseph.

Library of Congress Cataloging-in-Publication Data

Ensler, Eve.
The vagina monologues / Eve Ensler.
p.   cm.
ISBN 0-375-75052-5 (acid-free paper)
1. Monologues.   2. Vagina.   3. Women.   I. Title.
PS3555.N75V3   1998
812'.54—dc21   97-29393

Random House website address: www.randomhouse.com
Printed in the United States of America on acid-free paper

7986

Book design by Caroline Cunningham

For Ariel, who rocks my vagina

and explodes my heart

I come from the "down there" generation. That is, those were the words—spoken rarely and in a hushed voice—that the women in my family used to refer to all female genitalia, internal or external.

It wasn't that they were ignorant of terms like *vagina, labia, vulva,* or *clitoris.* On the contrary, they were trained to be teachers and probably had more access to information than most.

It wasn't even that they were unliberated, or "straitlaced," as they would have put it. One grandmother earned money from her strict Protestant church by ghostwriting sermons—of which she didn't believe a word—and then earned more by betting it on horse races. The other was a suffragist, educator, and even an early political candidate, all to the alarm of many in her Jewish community. As for my own mother, she had been a pioneer newspaper reporter years before I was born, and continued to take pride in bringing up her two daughters in a more enlightened way than she had been raised. I don't remember her using any of the slang words that made the female body seem dirty or shameful, and I'm grateful for that. As you'll see in these pages, many daughters grew up with a greater burden.

Nonetheless, I didn't hear words that were accurate, much less prideful. For example, I never once heard the word *clitoris.* It would be years before I learned that females possessed the only organ in the human body with no function other than to feel pleasure. (If such an organ were unique to the male body, can you imagine how much we would hear about it—and what it would be used to justify?) Thus, whether I was learning to talk, to spell, or to take care of my own body, I was told the name of each of its amazing parts— except in one unmentionable area. This left me unprotected against the shaming words and dirty jokes of the school yard and, later, against the popular belief that men, whether as lovers or physicians, knew more about women's bodies than women did.

I first glimpsed the spirit of self-knowledge and freedom that you will find in these pages when I lived in India for a couple of years after college. In Hindu temples and shrines I saw the lingam, an abstract male genital symbol, but I also saw the yoni, a female genital symbol, for the first time: a flowerlike shape, triangle, or double-pointed oval. I was told that thousands of years ago, this symbol had been worshiped as more powerful than its male counterpart, a belief that carried over into Tantrism, whose central tenet is man's inability to reach spiritual fulfillment except through sexual and emotional union with woman's superior spiritual energy. It was a belief so deep and wide that even some of the woman-excluding, monotheistic religions that came later retained it in their traditions, although such beliefs were (and still are) marginalized or denied as heresies by mainstream religious leaders.

For example: Gnostic Christians worshiped Sophia as the female Holy Spirit and considered Mary Magdalene the wisest of Christ's disciples; Tantric Buddhism still teaches that Buddhahood resides in the vulva; the Sufi mystics of Islam believe that *fana,* or rapture, can be reached only through Fravashi, the female spirit; the Shekina of Jewish mysticism is a version of Shakti, the female soul of God; and even the Catholic church included forms of Mary worship that focused more on the Mother than on the Son. In many countries of Asia, Africa, and other parts of the world where gods are still depicted in female as well as in male forms, altars feature the Jewel in the Lotus and other representations of the lingam-in-the-yoni. In India, the Hindu goddesses Durga and Kali are embodiments of the yoni powers of birth and death, creation and destruction.

Still, India and yoni worship seemed a long way from American attitudes about women's bodies when I came home. Even the sexual revolution of the 1960s only made more women sexually available to more men. The "no" of the 1950s was just replaced with a constant, eager "yes." It was not until the feminist activism of the 1970s that there began to be alternatives to everything from patriarchal religions to Freud (the distance from A to B), from the double standard of sexual behavior to the single standard of patriarchal/political/religious control over women's bodies as the means of reproduction.

Those early years of discovery are symbolized for me by such sense memories as walking through Judy Chicago's *Woman House* in Los Angeles, where each room was created by a different

woman artist, and where I discovered female sym-
bolism in my own culture for the first time. (For
example, the shape we call a heart—whose sym-
metry resembles the vulva far more than the
asymmetry of the organ that shares its name—is
probably a residual female genital symbol. It was
reduced from power to romance by centuries of
male dominance.) Or sitting in a New York coffee
shop with Betty Dodson (you will meet her in
these pages), trying to act cool while she electri-
fied eavesdroppers with her cheerful explanation
of masturbation as a liberating force. Or coming
back to *Ms.* magazine to find, among the always
humorous signs on its bulletin board: IT'S 10
O'CLOCK AT NIGHT—DO YOU KNOW WHERE YOUR
CLITORIS IS? By the time feminists were putting
CUNT POWER! on buttons and T-shirts as a way of
reclaiming that devalued word, I could recognize
the restoration of an ancient power. After all, the
Indo-European word *cunt* was derived from the
goddess Kali's title of Kunda or Cunti, and shares
the same root as *kin* and *country.*

These last three decades of feminism were also marked by a deep anger as the truth of violence against the female body was revealed, whether it took the form of rape, childhood sexual abuse, anti-lesbian violence, physical abuse of women, sexual harassment, terrorism against reproductive freedom, or the international crime of female genital mutilation. Women's sanity was saved by bringing these hidden experiences into the open, naming them, and turning our rage into positive action to reduce and heal violence. Part of the tidal wave of creativity that has resulted from this energy of truth telling is this play and book.

When I first went to see Eve Ensler perform the intimate narratives in these pages—gathered from more than two hundred interviews and then turned into poetry for the theater—I thought: *I already know this: it's the journey of truth telling we've been on for the past three decades.* And it is. Women have entrusted her with their most intimate experiences, from sex to birthing, from the undeclared war against women to the new freedom of love between women. On every page, there is the power of saying the unsayable—as there is in the behind-the-scenes story of the book itself. One publisher paid an advance for it, then, on sober second thought, allowed Eve Ensler to keep the money if she would take the book and its v-word elsewhere. (Thank Villard for publishing all of women's words—even in the title.)

But the value of *The Vagina Monologues* goes beyond purging a past full of negative attitudes. It offers a personal, grounded-in-the-body way of moving toward the future. I think readers, men as well as women, may emerge from these pages not only feeling more free within themselves—and about each other—but with alternatives to the old patriarchal dualism of feminine/masculine, body/mind, and sexual/spiritual that is rooted in the division of our physical selves into "the part we talk about" and "the part we don't."

If a book with *vagina* in the title still seems a long way from such questions of philosophy and politics, I offer one more of my belated discoveries.

In the 1970s, while researching in the Library of Congress, I found an obscure history of religious architecture that assumed a fact as if it were common knowledge: the traditional design of most patriarchal buildings of worship imitates the female body. Thus, there is an outer and inner entrance, labia majora and labia minora; a central vaginal aisle toward the altar; two curved ovarian structures on either side; and then in the sacred center, the altar or womb, where the miracle takes place—where males give birth.

Though this comparison was new to me, it struck home like a rock down a well. *Of course,* I thought. *The central ceremony of patriarchal religions is one in which men take over the yoni-power of creation by giving birth symbolically. No wonder male religious leaders so often say that humans were born in sin— because we were born to female creatures. Only by obeying the rules of the patriarchy can we be reborn through men. No wonder priests and ministers in skirts sprinkle imitation birth fluid over our heads, give us new names, and promise rebirth into everlasting life. No wonder the male priesthood tries to keep women away from the altar, just as women are kept away from control of our own powers of reproduction. Symbolic or real, it's all devoted to controlling the power that resides in the female body.*

Since then, I've never felt the same estrangement when entering a patriarchal religious structure. Instead, I walk down the vaginal aisle, plotting to take back the altar with priests—female as well as male—who would not disparage female sexuality, to universalize the male-only myths of Creation, to multiply spiritual words and symbols, and to restore the spirit of God in all living things.

If overthrowing some five thousand years of patriarchy seems like a big order, just focus on celebrating each self-respecting step along the way.

I thought of this while watching little girls drawing hearts in their notebooks, even dotting their *i*'s with hearts, and I wondered: *Were they magnetized by this primordial shape because it was so like their own bodies?* I thought of it again while listening to a group of twenty or so diverse nine- to sixteen-year-old girls as they decided to come up with a collective word that included everything— vagina, labia, clitoris. After much discussion, "power bundle" was their favorite. More important, the discussion was carried on with shouts and laughter. I thought: *What a long and blessed way from a hushed "down there."*

I wish my own foremothers had known their bodies were sacred. With the help of outrageous voices and honest words like those in this book, I believe the grandmothers, mothers, and daughters of the future will heal their selves—and mend the world.

INTRODUCTION

"Vagina." There, I've said it. "Vagina"—said it again. I've been saying that word over and over for the last three years. I've been saying it in theaters, at colleges, in living rooms, in cafés, at dinner parties, on radio programs all over the country. I would be saying it on TV if someone would let me. I say it one hundred and twenty-eight times every evening I perform my show, *The Vagina Monologues,* which is based on interviews with a diverse group of over two hundred women about their vaginas. I say it in my sleep. I say it because I'm not supposed to say it. I say it because it's an invisible word—a word that stirs up anxiety, awkwardness, contempt, and disgust.

I say it because I believe that what we don't say we don't see, acknowledge, or remember. What we don't say becomes a secret, and secrets often create shame and fear and myths. I say it because I want to someday feel comfortable saying it, and not ashamed and guilty.

I say it because we haven't come up with a word that's more inclusive, that really describes the entire area and all its parts. "Pussy" is probably a better word, but it has so much baggage connected with it. And besides, I don't think most of us have a clear idea of what we're talking about when we say "pussy." "Vulva" is a good word; it speaks more specifically, but I don't think most of us are clear what the vulva includes.

I say "vagina" because when I started saying it I discovered how fragmented I was, how disconnected my body was from my mind. My vagina was something over there, away in the distance. I rarely lived inside it, or even visited. I was busy working, writing; being a mother, a friend. I did not see my vagina as my primary resource, a place of sustenance, humor, and creativity. It was fraught there, full of fear. I'd been raped as a little girl, and although I'd grown up, and done all the adult things one does with one's vagina, I had never really reentered that part of my body after I'd been violated. I had essentially lived most of my life without my motor, my center, my second heart.

I say "vagina" because I want people to respond, and they have. They have tried to censor the word wherever *The Vagina Monologues* has traveled and in every form of communication: in ads in major newspapers, on tickets sold in department stores, on banners that hang in front of theaters, on box-office phone machines where the voice says only "Monologues" or "V. Monologues."

"Why is this?" I ask. " 'Vagina' is not a pornographic word; it's actually a medical word, a term for a body part, like 'elbow,' 'hand,' or 'rib.' "

"It may not be pornographic," people say, "but it's dirty. What if our little daughters were to hear it, what would we tell them?"

"Maybe you could tell them that they have a vagina," I say. "If they don't already know it. Maybe you could celebrate that."

"But we don't call their vaginas 'vagina,' " they say.

"What do you call them?" I ask.

And they tell me: "pooki," "poochie," "poope," "peepe poopelu" . . . and the list goes on and on.

I say "vagina" because I have read the statistics, and bad things are happening to women's vaginas everywhere: 500,000 women are raped every year in the United States; 100 million women have been genitally mutilated worldwide; and the list goes on and on. I say "vagina" because I want these bad things to stop. I know they will not stop until we acknowledge that they're going on, and the only way to make that possible is to enable women to talk without fear of punishment or retribution.

It's scary saying the word. "Vagina." At first it feels like you're crashing through an invisible wall. "Vagina." You feel guilty and wrong, as if someone's going to strike you down. Then, after you say the word the hundredth time or the thousandth time, it occurs to you that it's *your* word, *your* body, *your* most essential place. You suddenly realize that all the shame and embarrassment you've previously felt saying the word has been a form of silencing your desire, eroding your ambition.

Then you begin to say the word more and more. You say it with a kind of passion, a kind of urgency, because you sense that if you stop saying it, the fear will overcome you again and you will fall back into an embarrassed whisper. So you say it everywhere you can, bring it up in every conversation.

You're excited about your vagina; you want to study it and explore it and introduce yourself to it, and find out how to listen to it, and give it pleasure, and keep it healthy and wise and strong. You learn how to satisfy yourself and teach your lover how to satisfy you.

You're aware of your vagina all day, wherever you are—in your car, at the supermarket, at the gym, in the office. You're aware of this precious, gorgeous, life-bearing part of you between your legs, and it makes you smile; it makes you proud.

And as more women say the word, saying it becomes less of a big deal; it becomes part of our language, part of our lives. Our vaginas become integrated and respected and sacred. They become part of our bodies, connected to our minds, fueling our spirits. And the shame leaves and the violation stops, because vaginas are visible and real, and they are connected to powerful, wise, vagina-talking women.

We have a huge journey in front of us.

This is the beginning. Here's the place to

think about our vaginas, to learn about other women's vaginas, to hear stories and interviews, to answer questions and to ask them. Here's the place to release the myths, shame, and fear. Here's the place to practice saying the word, because, as we know, the word is what propels us and sets us free. "VAGINA."

THE
VAGINA
MONOLOGUES

I bet you're worried. *I* was worried. That's
why I began this piece. I was worried about vaginas. I was worried about what we think about
vaginas, and even more worried that we don't
think about them. I was worried about my own
vagina. It needed a context of other vaginas—a
community, a culture of vaginas. There's so much
darkness and secrecy surrounding them—like the

Bermuda Triangle. Nobody ever reports back from there.

In the first place, it's not so easy even to find your vagina. Women go weeks, months, sometimes years without looking at it. I interviewed a high-powered businesswoman who told me she was too busy; she didn't have the time. Looking at your vagina, she said, is a full day's work. You have to get down there on your back in front of a mirror that's standing on its own, full-length preferred. You've got to get in the perfect position, with the perfect light, which then is shadowed somehow by the mirror and the angle you're at. You get all twisted up. You're arching your head up, killing your back. You're exhausted by then. She said she didn't have the time for that. She was busy.

So I decided to talk to women about their vaginas, to do vagina interviews, which became vagina monologues. I talked with over two hundred women. I talked to old women, young women, married women, single women, lesbians, college professors, actors, corporate professionals, sex workers, African American women, Hispanic women, Asian American women, Native American women, Caucasion women, Jewish women. At first women were reluctant to talk. They were a little shy. But once they got going, you couldn't stop them. Women secretly love to talk about their vaginas. They get very excited, mainly because no one's ever asked them before.

Let's just start with the word "vagina." It sounds like an infection at best, maybe a medical instrument: "Hurry, Nurse, bring me the vagina." "Vagina." "Vagina." Doesn't matter how many times you say it, it never sounds like a word you want to say. It's a totally ridiculous, completely unsexy word. If you use it during sex, trying to be politically correct—"Darling, could you stroke my vagina?"—you kill the act right there.

I'm worried about vaginas, what we call them and don't call them.

In Great Neck, they call it a pussycat. A woman there told me that her mother used to tell her, "Don't wear panties underneath your pajamas, dear; you need to air out your pussycat." In Westchester they called it a pooki, in New Jersey a twat. There's "powderbox," "derrière," a "poochi," a "poopi," a "peepe," a "poopelu," a "poonani," a "pal" and a "piche," "toadie," "dee dee," "nishi," "dignity," "monkey box," "coochi snorcher," "cooter," "labbe," "Gladys Siegelman," "VA," "wee wee," "horsespot," "nappy dugout," "mongo," a "pajama," "fannyboo," "mushmellow," a "ghoulie," "possible," "tamale," "tottita," "Connie," a "Mimi" in Miami, "split knish" in Philadelphia, and "schmende" in the Bronx. I am worried about vaginas.

Some of the monologues are close to verbatim inter-views, some are composite interviews, and with some I just began with the seed of an interview and had a good time. This monologue is pretty much the way I heard it. Its subject, however, came up in every interview, and often it was fraught. The subject being

H A I R

You cannot love a vagina unless you love hair. Many people do not love hair. My first and only husband hated hair. He said it was cluttered and dirty. He made me shave my vagina. It looked puffy and exposed and like a little girl. This excited him. When he made love to me, my vagina felt the way a beard must feel. It felt good to rub it, and painful. Like scratching a mosquito bite. It felt like it was on fire. There were screaming red

9

bumps. I refused to shave it again. Then my husband had an affair. When we went to marital therapy, he said he screwed around because I wouldn't please him sexually. I wouldn't shave my vagina. The therapist had a thick German accent and gasped between sentences to show her empathy. She asked me why I didn't want to please my husband. I told her I thought it was weird. I felt little when my hair was gone down there, and I couldn't help talking in a baby voice, and the skin got irritated and even calamine lotion wouldn't help it. She told me marriage was a compromise. I asked her if shaving my vagina would stop him from screwing around. I asked her if she'd had many cases like this before. She said that questions diluted the process. I needed to jump in. She was sure it was a good beginning.

This time, when we got home, he got to shave my vagina. It was like a therapy bonus prize. He clipped it a few times, and there was a little blood in the bathtub. He didn't even notice it, 'cause he was so happy shaving me. Then, later, when my husband was pressing against me, I could feel his spiky sharpness sticking into me, my naked puffy vagina. There was no protection. There was no fluff.

I realized then that hair is there for a reason—it's the leaf around the flower, the lawn around the house. You have to love hair in order to love the vagina. You can't pick the parts you want. And besides, my husband never stopped screwing around.

I asked all the women I interviewed the same questions and then I picked my favorite answers. Although I must tell you, I've never heard an answer I didn't love. I asked women:

"If your vagina got dressed, what would it wear?"

A leather jacket.

Silk stockings.

Mink.

A pink boa.

A male tuxedo.

Jeans.

Something formfitting.

Emeralds.

An evening gown.

Sequins.

Armani only.

A tutu.

See-through black underwear.

A taffeta ball gown.

Something machine washable.

Costume eye mask.

Purple velvet pajamas.

Angora.

A red bow.

Ermine and pearls.

A large hat full of flowers.

A leopard hat.

A silk kimono.

A beret.

Sweatpants.

A tattoo.

An electrical shock device to keep unwanted
strangers away.

High heels.

Lace *and* combat boots.

Purple feathers and twigs and shells.

Cotton.

A pinafore.

A bikini.

A slicker.

"If your vagina could talk, what would it say, in two words?"

Slow down.
Is that you?
Feed me.
I want.
Yum, yum.
Oh, yeah.

Start again.

No, over there.

Lick me.

Stay home.

Brave choice.

Think again.

More, please.

Embrace me.

Let's play.

Don't stop.

More, more.

Remember me?

Come inside.

Not yet.

Whoah, Mama.

Yes yes.

Rock me.

Enter at your own risk.

Oh, God.

Thank God.

I'm here.

Let's go.

Let's go.

Find me.

Thank you.

Bonjour.

Too hard.

Don't give up.

Where's Brian?

That's better.

Yes, there. There.

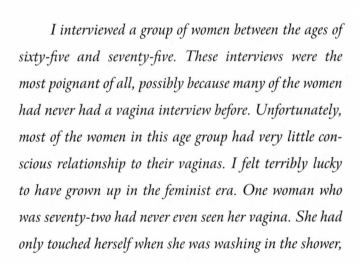

I interviewed a group of women between the ages of sixty-five and seventy-five. These interviews were the most poignant of all, possibly because many of the women had never had a vagina interview before. Unfortunately, most of the women in this age group had very little conscious relationship to their vaginas. I felt terribly lucky to have grown up in the feminist era. One woman who was seventy-two had never even seen her vagina. She had only touched herself when she was washing in the shower,

but never with conscious intention. She had never had an orgasm. At seventy-two she went into therapy, and with the encouragement of her therapist, she went home one afternoon by herself, lit some candles, took a bath, played some comforting music, and discovered her vagina. She said it took her over an hour, because she was arthritic by then, but when she finally found her clitoris, she said, she cried. This monologue is for her.

THE FLOOD

[Jewish, Queens accent]

Down there? I haven't been down there since
1953. No, it had nothing to do with Eisenhower.
No, no, it's a cellar down there. It's very damp,
clammy. You don't want to go down there. Trust
me. You'd get sick. Suffocating. Very nauseating.
The smell of the clamminess and the mildew and
everything. Whew! Smells unbearable. Gets in
your clothes.

No, there was no accident down there. It

didn't blow up or catch on fire or anything. It wasn't so dramatic. I mean . . . well, never mind. No. Never mind. I can't talk to you about this. What's a smart girl like you going around talking to old ladies about their down-theres for? We didn't do this kind of a thing when I was a girl. What? Jesus, okay.

There was this boy, Andy Leftkov. He was cute—well, I thought so. And tall, like me, and I really liked him. He asked me out for a date in his car. . . .

I can't tell you this. I can't do this, talk about down there. You just know it's there. Like the cellar. There's rumbles down there sometimes. You can hear the pipes, and things get caught there, little animals and things, and it gets wet, and sometimes people have to come and plug up the leaks. Otherwise, the door stays closed. You forget about it. I mean, it's part of the house, but you don't see it or think about it. It has to be there, though, 'cause every house needs a cellar. Otherwise the bedroom would be in the basement.

Oh, Andy, Andy Leftkov. Right. Andy was very good-looking. He was a catch. That's what we called it in my day. We were in his car, a new white Chevy BelAir. I remember thinking that my legs were too long for the seat. I have long legs. They were bumping up against the dashboard. I was looking at my big kneecaps when he just kissed me in this surprisingly "Take me by control like they do in the movies" kind of way. And I got excited, so excited, and, well, there was a flood down there. I couldn't control it. It was like this force of passion, this river of life just flooded out of me, right through my panties, right onto the car seat of his new white Chevy BelAir. It wasn't pee and it was smelly—well, frankly, I didn't really smell anything at all, but he said, Andy said, that it smelled like sour milk and it was staining his car seat. I was "a stinky weird girl," he said. I wanted to explain that his kiss had caught me off guard, that I wasn't normally like this. I tried to wipe the flood up with my dress. It was a new yellow prim-rose dress and it looked so ugly with the flood on it. Andy drove me home and he never, never said another word and when I got out and closed his car door, I closed the whole store. Locked it. Never opened for business again. I dated some after that, but the idea of flooding made me too nervous. I never even got close again.

I used to have dreams, crazy dreams. Oh, they're dopey. Why? Burt Reynolds. I don't know why. He never did much for me in life, but in my dreams . . . it was always Burt. It was always the same general dream. We'd be out. Burt and I. It was some restaurant like the kind you see in Atlantic City, all big with chandeliers and stuff and thousands of waiters with vests on. Burt would give me this orchid corsage. I'd pin it on my blazer. We'd laugh. Eat shrimp cocktail. Huge shrimp, fabulous shrimp. We'd laugh more. We were very happy together. Then he'd look into my eyes and pull me to him in the middle of the restaurant—and, just as he was about to kiss me, the room would start to shake, pigeons would fly out from under the table—I don't know what those pigeons were doing there—and the flood would come straight from down there. It would pour out of me. It would pour and pour. There would be fish inside it, and little boats, and the whole restaurant would fill with water, and Burt would be standing knee-deep in my flood, looking horribly disappointed in me that I'd done it again, horrified as he watched his friends, Dean Martin and the like, swim past us in their tuxedos and evening gowns.

I don't have those dreams anymore. Not since they took away just about everything connected with down there. Moved out the uterus, the tubes, the whole works. The doctor thought he was being funny. He told me if you don't use it, you lose it. But really I found out it was cancer. Everything around it had to go. Who needs it, anyway? Right? Highly overrated. I've done other things. I love the dog shows. I sell antiques.

What would it wear? What kind of question is that? What would it wear? It would wear a big sign:

"Closed Due to Flooding."

What would it say? I told you. It's not like that. It's not like a person who speaks. It stopped being a thing that talked a long time ago. It's a place. A place you don't go. It's closed up, under the house. It's down there. You happy? You made me talk—you got it out of me. You got an old lady to talk about her down-there. You feel better now? [Turns away; turns back.]

You know, actually, you're the first person I ever talked to about this, and I feel a little better.

VAGINA FACT

At a witch trial in 1593, the investigating lawyer (a married man) apparently discovered a clitoris for the first time; [he] identified it as a devil's teat, sure proof of the witch's guilt. It was "a little lump of flesh, in manner sticking out as if it had been a teat, to the length of half an inch," which the gaoler, "perceiving at the first sight thereof, meant not to disclose, because it was adjoining to so secret a place which was not decent to be seen. Yet in the end, not willing to conceal so strange a matter," he showed it to various by-standers. The bystanders had never seen anything like it. The witch was convicted.

—*The Woman's Encyclopedia of Myths and Secrets*

I interviewed many women about menstruation. There was a choral thing that began to occur, a kind of wild collective song. Women echoed each other. I let the voices bleed into one another. I got lost in the bleeding.

I WAS TWELVE. MY MOTHER SLAPPED ME.

Second grade, seven years old, my brother was talking about periods. I didn't like the way he was laughing.

I went to my mother. "What's a period?" I said. "It's punctuation," she said. "You put it at the end of a sentence."

My father brought me a card: "To my little girl who isn't so little anymore."

I was terrified. My mother showed me the

thick sanitary napkins. I was to bring the used ones to the can under the kitchen sink.

I remember being one of the last. I was thirteen.

We all wanted it to come.

I was so afraid. I started putting the used pads in brown paper bags in the dark storage places under the roof.

Eighth grade. My mother said, "Oh, that's nice."

In junior high—brown drips before it came. Coincided with a little hair under my arms, which grew unevenly: one armpit had hair, the other didn't.

I was sixteen, sort of scared.

My mother gave me codeine. We had bunk beds. I went down and lay there. My mother was so uncomfortable.

One night, I came home late and snuck into bed without turning on any lights. My mother had found the used pads and put them between the sheets of my bed.

I was twelve years old, still in my underpants. Hadn't gotten dressed. Looked down on the staircase. There it was.

Looked down and I saw blood.

Seventh grade; my mother sort of noticed my underwear. Then she gave me plastic diapers.

My mom was very warm—"Let's get you a pad."

My friend Marcia, they celebrated when she got hers. They had dinner for her.

We all wanted our period.

We all wanted it *now*.

Thirteen years old. It was before Kotex. Had to watch your dress. I was black and poor. Blood on the back of my dress in church. Didn't show, but I was guilty.

I was ten and a half. No preparation. Brown gunk on my underpants.

She showed me how to put in a tampon. Only got in halfway.

I associated my period with inexplicable phenomena.

My mother told me I had to use a rag. My mother said no to tampons. You couldn't put anything in your sugar dish.

Wore wads of cotton. Told my mother. She gave me Elizabeth Taylor paper dolls.

Fifteen years old. My mother said, "Mazel tov." She slapped me in the face. Didn't know if it was a good thing or a bad thing.

My period, like cake mix before it's baked. Indians sat on moss for five days. Wish I were Native American.

I was fifteen and I'd been hoping to get it. I was tall and I kept growing.

When I saw white girls in the gym with tampons, I thought they were bad girls.

Saw little red drops on the pink tiles. I said, "Yeah."

My mom was glad for me.

Used OB and liked putting my fingers up there.

Eleven years old, wearing white pants. Blood started to come out.

Thought it was dreadful.

I'm not ready.

I got back pains.

I got horny.

Twelve years old. I was happy. My friend had a Ouija board, asked when we were going to get our periods, looked down, and I saw blood.

Looked down and there it was.

I'm a woman.

Terrified.

Never thought it would come.

Changed my whole feeling about myself. I became very silent and mature. A good Vietnamese woman—quiet worker, virtuous, never speaks.

Nine and a half. I was sure I was bleeding to death, rolled up my underwear and threw them in a corner. Didn't want to worry my parents.

My mother made me hot water and wine, and I fell asleep.

I was in my bedroom in my mother's apartment. I had a comic book collection. My mother said, "You mustn't lift your box of comic books."

My girlfriends told me you hemorrhage every month.

My mother was in and out of mental hospitals. She couldn't take me coming of age.

"Dear Miss Carling, Please excuse my daughter from basketball. She has just matured."

At camp they told me not to take a bath with my period. They wiped me down with antiseptic.

Scared people would smell it. Scared they'd say I smelled like fish.

Throwing up, couldn't eat.

I got hungry.

Sometimes it's very red.

I like the drops that drop into the toilet. Like paint.

Sometimes it's brown and it disturbs me.

I was twelve. My mother slapped me and brought me a red cotton shirt. My father went out for a bottle of sangria.

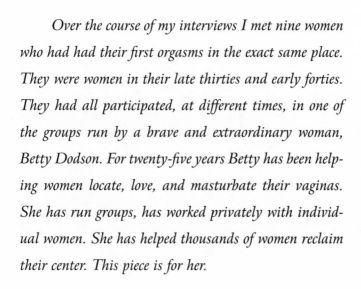

Over the course of my interviews I met nine women who had had their first orgasms in the exact same place. They were women in their late thirties and early forties. They had all participated, at different times, in one of the groups run by a brave and extraordinary woman, Betty Dodson. For twenty-five years Betty has been help-ing women locate, love, and masturbate their vaginas. She has run groups, has worked privately with individ-ual women. She has helped thousands of women reclaim their center. This piece is for her.

THE
VAGINA
WORKSHOP

[A slight English accent]

My vagina is a shell, a round pink tender shell,
opening and closing, closing and opening. My vagina is
a flower, an eccentric tulip, the center acute and deep, the
scent delicate, the petals gentle but sturdy.

I did not always know this. I learned this in
the vagina workshop. I learned this from a woman
who runs the vagina workshop, a woman who be-

lieves in vaginas, who really sees vaginas, who helps women see their own vaginas by seeing other women's vaginas.

In the first session the woman who runs the vagina workshop asked us to draw a picture of our own "unique, beautiful, fabulous vagina." That's what she called it. She wanted to know what our own unique, beautiful, fabulous vagina looked like to us. One woman who was pregnant drew a big red mouth screaming with coins spilling out. Another very skinny woman drew a big serving plate with a kind of Devonshire pattern on it. I drew a huge black dot with little squiggly lines around it. The black dot was equal to a black hole in space, and the squiggly lines were meant to be people or things or just your basic atoms that got lost there. I had always thought of my vagina as an anatomical vacuum randomly sucking up particles and objects from the surrounding environment.

I had always perceived my vagina as an independent entity, spinning like a star in its own galaxy, eventually burning up on its own gaseous energy or exploding and splitting into thousands of other smaller vaginas, all of them then spinning in their own galaxies.

I did not think of my vagina in practical or biological terms. I did not, for example, see it as a part of my body, something between my legs, attached to me.

In the workshop we were asked to look at our vaginas with hand mirrors. Then, after careful examination, we were to verbally report to the group what we saw. I must tell you that up until this point everything I knew about my vagina was based on hearsay or invention. I had never really seen the thing. It had never occurred to me to look at it. My vagina existed for me on some abstract plane. It seemed so reductive and awkward to look at it, getting down there the way we did in the workshop, on our shiny blue mats, with our hand mirrors. It reminded me of how the early astronomers must have felt with their primitive telescopes.

I found it quite unsettling at first, my vagina.

Like the first time you see a fish cut open and you discover this other bloody complex world inside, right under the skin. It was so raw, so red, so fresh. And the thing that surprised me most was all the layers. Layers inside layers, opening into more layers. My vagina, like some mystical event that keeps unfolding another aspect of itself, which is really an event in itself, but you only know it after the event.

My vagina amazed me. I couldn't speak when it came my turn in the workshop. I was speechless. I had awakened to what the woman who ran the workshop called "vaginal wonder." I just wanted to lie there on my mat, my legs spread, examining my vagina forever.

It was better than the Grand Canyon, ancient and full of grace. It had the innocence and freshness of a proper English garden. It was funny, very funny. It made me laugh. It could hide and seek, open and close. It was a mouth. It was the morning. And then it momentarily occurred to me that it was *me,* my vagina: it was who *I* was. It was not an entity. It was inside of me.

Then, the woman who ran the workshop asked how many women in the workshop had had orgasms. Two women tentatively raised their hands. I didn't raise my hand, but I had had orgasms. I didn't raise my hand because they were accidental orgasms. They happened *to* me. They happened in my dreams, and I would wake in splendor. They happened a lot in water, mostly in the bath. Once in Cape Cod. They happened on horses, on bicycles, on the treadmill at the gym. I did not raise my hand because although I had had orgasms, I did not know how to make one happen. I had never tried to make one happen. I thought it was a mystical, magical thing. I didn't want to interfere. It felt wrong, getting involved— contrived, manipulative. It felt Hollywood. Orgasms by formula. The surprise would be gone, and the mystery. The problem, of course, was that the surprise had been gone for two years. I hadn't had a magical accidental orgasm in a long time, and I was frantic. That's why I was in the workshop.

And then the moment had arrived that I both dreaded and secretly longed for. The woman who ran the workshop asked us to take out our hand mirrors again and to see if we could locate our clitoris. We were there, the group of us women, on our backs, on our mats, finding our spots, our locus, our reason, and I don't know why, but I started crying. Maybe it was sheer embarrassment. Maybe it was knowing that I had to give up the fantasy, the enormous life-consuming fantasy, that someone or something was going to do this for me—the fantasy that someone was coming to lead my life, to choose direction, to give me orgasms. I was used to living off the record, in a magical, superstitious way. This clitoris finding, this wild workshop on shiny blue mats, was making the whole thing real, too real. I could feel the panic coming. The simultaneous terror and realization that I had avoided finding my clitoris, had rationalized it as mainstream and consumerist because I was, in fact, terrified that I did not *have* a clitoris, terrified that I was one of those constitutionally incapables, one of those frigid, dead, shutdown, dry, apricot-tasting, bitter—oh, my God. I lay there with my mirror looking for my spot, reaching with my fingers, and all I could think about was the time when I was ten and lost my gold ring with the emeralds in a lake. How I kept diving over and over to the bottom of the lake, running my hands over stones and fish and bottle caps and slimy stuff, but never my ring. The panic I felt. I knew I'd be punished. I shouldn't have worn it swimming.

The woman who ran the workshop saw my insane scrambling, sweating, and heavy breathing. She came over. I told her, "I've lost my clitoris. It's gone. I shouldn't have worn it swimming." The woman who ran the workshop laughed. She calmly stroked my forehead. She told me my clitoris was not something I could lose. It was me, the essence of me. It was both the doorbell to my house and the house itself. I didn't have to *find* it. I had to *be* it. Be it. Be my vagina. Be my vagina. I lay back and closed my eyes. I put the mirror down. I watched myself float above myself. I watched as I slowly began to approach myself and reenter. I felt like an astronaut reentering the atmosphere of the earth. It was very quiet, this reentry: quiet and gentle. I bounced and landed, landed and bounced. I came into my own muscles and blood and cells and then I just slid into my vagina. It was suddenly easy and I fit. I was all warm and pulsing and ready and young and alive. And then, without looking, with my eyes still closed, I put my finger on what had suddenly become me. There was a little quivering at first, which urged me to stay. Then the quivering became a quake, an eruption, the layers dividing and subdividing. The quaking broke open into an ancient horizon of light and silence, which opened onto a plane of music and colors and innocence and longing, and I felt connection, calling connection as I lay there thrashing about on my little blue mat.

My vagina is a shell, a tulip, and a destiny. I am arriving as I am beginning to leave. My vagina, my vagina, me.

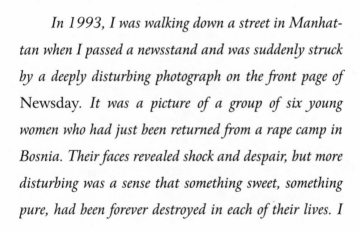

In 1993, I was walking down a street in Manhattan when I passed a newsstand and was suddenly struck by a deeply disturbing photograph on the front page of Newsday. *It was a picture of a group of six young women who had just been returned from a rape camp in Bosnia. Their faces revealed shock and despair, but more disturbing was a sense that something sweet, something pure, had been forever destroyed in each of their lives. I*

read on. Inside the newspaper was another photograph of the young women, recently reunited with their mothers and standing in a semicircle in a gymnasium. There was a very large group and not one of them, mother or daughter, was able to look at the camera.

I knew I had to go there. I had to meet these women. In 1994, thanks to the support of an angel, Lauren Lloyd, I spent two months in Croatia and Pakistan, interviewing Bosnian women refugees. I interviewed these women and hung out with them in camps, cafés, and refugee centers. I have been back to Bosnia twice since then.

When I returned to New York after my first trip, I was in a state of outrage. Outraged that 20,000 to 70,000 women were being raped in the middle of Europe in 1993, as a systematic tactic of war, and no one was doing anything to stop it. I couldn't understand it. A friend asked me why I was surprised. She said that over 500,000 women were raped every year in this country, and in theory we were not at war.

This monologue is based on one woman's story. I

want to thank her here for sharing it with me. I am in awe of her spirit and strength, as I am in awe of every woman I met who survived these terrible atrocities in the former Yugoslavia. This piece is for the women of Bosnia.

MY VAGINA WAS MY

VILLAGE

My vagina was green, water soft pink fields, cow mooing sun resting sweet boyfriend touching lightly with soft piece of blond straw.

There is something between my legs. I do not know what it is. I do not know where it is. I do not touch. Not now. Not anymore. Not since.

My vagina was chatty, can't wait, so much, so much saying, words talking, can't quit trying, can't quit saying, oh yes, oh yes.

Not since I dream there's a dead animal sewn in down there with thick black fishing line. And the bad dead animal smell cannot be removed. And its throat is slit and it bleeds through all my summer dresses.

My vagina singing all girl songs, all goat bells ringing songs, all wild autumn field songs, vagina songs, vagina home songs.

Not since the soldiers put a long thick rifle inside me. So cold, the steel rod canceling my heart. Don't know whether they're going to fire it or shove it through my spinning brain. Six of them, monstrous doctors with black masks shoving bottles up me too. There were sticks, and the end of a broom.

My vagina swimming river water, clean spilling water over sun-baked stones over stone clit, clit stones over and over.

Not since I heard the skin tear and made lemon screeching sounds, not since a piece of my vagina came off in my hand, a part of the lip, now one side of the lip is completely gone.

My vagina. A live wet water village. My vagina my hometown.

Not since they took turns for seven days smelling like feces and smoked meat, they left their dirty sperm inside me. I became a river of poison and pus and all the crops died, and the fish.

My vagina a live wet water village.

They invaded it. Butchered it and burned it
   down.

I do not touch now.

Do not visit.

I live someplace else now.

I don't know where that is.

In the nineteenth century, girls who learned to develop orgasmic capacity by masturbation were regarded as medical problems. Often they were "treated" or "corrected" by amputation or cautery of the clitoris or "miniature chastity belts," sewing the vaginal lips together to put the clitoris out of reach, and even castration by surgical removal of the ovaries. But there are no references in the medical literature to the surgical removal of testicles or amputation of the penis to stop masturbation in boys.

In the United States, the last recorded clitoridectomy for curing masturbation was performed in 1948—on a five-year-old girl.

—*The Woman's Encyclopedia of Myths and Secrets*

VAGINA FACT

Genital mutilation has been inflicted on 80 [million] to 100 million girls and young women. In countries where it is practiced, mostly African, about 2 million youngsters a year can expect the knife—or the razor or a glass shard—to cut their clitoris or remove it altogether, [and] to have part or all of the labia . . . sewn together with catgut or thorns.

Often the operation is prettified as "circumcision." The African specialist Nahid Toubia puts it plain: In a man it would range from amputation of most of the penis, to "removal of all the penis, its roots of soft tissue and part of the scrotal skin."

Short-term results include tetanus, septicemia, hemorrhages, cuts in the urethra, bladder, vaginal walls, and anal sphincter. Long-term: chronic uterine infection, massive scars that can hinder walking for life, fistula formation, hugely increased agony and danger during childbirth, and early deaths.

—*The New York Times,* April 12, 1996

*For the last ten years I have been actively involved
with women who have no homes, women we call "home-
less people" so we can categorize and forget them. I have
done all kinds of things with these women, who have become my friends. I run recovery groups for women who
have been raped or suffered incest, and groups for women
addicted to drugs and alcohol. I go to the movies with
these women, I have meals with them. I hang out. Over*

the past ten years I have interviewed hundreds of women. In all that time I have met only two who were not sub- jected to incest as young girls or raped as young women. I have evolved a theory that for most of these women, "home" is a very scary place, a place they have fled, and that the shelters where I meet them are the first places many of them ever find safety, protection, or comfort, in the community of other women.

This monologue is one woman's story as she told it to me. I met her about five years ago, in a shelter. I would like to tell you it's an unusual story—brutal; extreme. But it's not. In fact, it's not nearly as disturbing as many of the stories I've heard in the years since. Poor women suffer terrible sexual violence that goes unre- ported. Because of their social class, these women do not have access to therapy or other methods of healing. Their repeated abuse ultimately eats away at their self-esteem, driving them to drugs, prostitution, AIDS, and in many cases, death. Fortunately, this particular story has a different outcome. This woman met another woman in that shelter, and they fell in love. Through their love, they got out of the shelter system and have a beautiful life together today. I wrote this piece for them, for their amazing spirits, for the women we do not see, who hurt and who need us.

THE LITTLE COOCHI SNORCHER THAT COULD

[Southern woman of color]

Memory: December 1965; Five Years Old

My mama tells me in a scary, loud, life-threatening voice to stop scratching my coochi snorcher. I become terrified that I've scratched it off down there. I do not touch myself again, even in the bath. I am afraid of the water getting in and filling me up so I explode. I put Band-Aids over my coochi snorcher to cover the hole, but they fall off in the water. I imagine a stopper, a bathtub plug up there to prevent things from entering me. I sleep with three pairs of happy heart-patterned cotton underpants underneath my snap-up pajamas. I still want to touch myself, but I don't.

Memory: Seven Years Old

Edgar Montane, who is ten, gets angry at me and punches me with all his might between my legs. It feels like he breaks my entire self. I limp home. I can't pee. My mama asks me what's wrong with my coochi snorcher, and when I tell her what Edgar did to me she yells at me and says never to let anyone touch me down there again. I try to explain he didn't touch it, Mama, he punched it.

Memory: Nine Years Old

I play on the bed, bouncing and falling, and impale my coochi snorcher on the bedpost. I make high-pitched screamy noises that come straight from my coochi snorcher's mouth. I get taken to the hospital and they sew it up down there from where it's been torn apart.

Memory: Ten Years Old

I'm at my father's house and he's having a party upstairs. Everyone's drinking. I'm playing alone in the basement and I'm trying on my new white cotton bra and panties that my father's girlfriend gave me. Suddenly my father's best friend, this big man Alfred, comes up from behind and pulls my new underpants down and sticks his big hard penis into my coochi scorcher. I scream. I kick. I try to fight him off, but he already gets it in. My father's there then and he has a gun and there's a loud horrible noise and then there's blood all over Alfred and me, lots of blood. I'm sure my coochi snorcher is finally falling out. Alfred is paralyzed for life and my mama doesn't let me see my father for seven years.

Memory: Twelve Years Old

My coochi snorcher is a very bad place, a place of pain, nastiness, punching, invasion, and blood. It's a site for mishaps. It's a bad-luck zone. I imagine a freeway between my legs and, girl, I am traveling, going far away from here.

Memory: Thirteen Years Old

There's this gorgeous twenty-four-year-old woman in our neighborhood and I stare at her all the time. One day she invites me into her car. She asks me if I like to kiss boys, and I tell her I do not like that. Then she says she wants to show me something, and she leans over and kisses me so softly on the lips with her lips and then puts her tongue in my mouth. Wow. She asks me if I want to come over to her house, and then she kisses me again and tells me to relax, to feel it, to let our tongues feel it. She asks my mama if I can spend the night and my mother's delighted that such a beautiful, successful woman has taken an interest in me. I'm scared and I can't wait. Her apartment's fantastic. She's got it hooked up. It's the seventies: the beads, the fluffy pillows, the mood lights. I decide right there that I want to be a secretary like her when I grow up. She makes a vodka for herself and then she asks what I want to drink. I say the same as she's drinking and she says she doesn't think my mama would like me drinking vodka. I say she probably wouldn't like me kissing girls, either, and the pretty lady makes me a drink. Then she changes into this chocolate satin teddy. She's so beautiful. I always thought bulldaggers were ugly. I say, "You look great," and she says, "So do you." I say, "But I only have this white cotton bra and underpants." Then she dresses me, slowly, in another satin teddy. It's lavender like the first soft days of spring. The alcohol has gone to my head and I'm loose and ready. There's a picture over her bed of a naked black woman with a huge afro. She gently and slowly lays me out on the bed and just our bodies rubbing makes me come. Then she does everything to me and my coochi snorcher that I always thought was nasty before, and wow. I'm so hot, so wild. She says, "Your vagina, untouched by man, smells so nice, so fresh, wish I could keep it that way forever." I get crazy wild and then the phone rings and of course it's my mama. I'm sure she knows; she catches me at everything. I'm breathing so heavy and I try to act normal when I get on the phone and she asks me, "What's wrong with you, have you been running?" I say, "No, Mama, exercising." Then she tells the beautiful secretary to make sure I'm not around boys and the lady tells her, "Trust me, there's no boys around here." Afterward the gorgeous lady teaches me everything about my coochi snorcher. She makes me play with myself in front of her and she teaches me all the different ways to give myself pleasure. She's very thorough. She tells me to always know how to give myself pleasure so I'll never need to rely on a man. In the morning I am worried that I've become a butch because I'm so in love with her. She laughs, but I never see her again. Now people say that it was a kind of rape. I was only thirteen and she was twenty-four. Well, I say, if it was a rape, it was a good rape then, a rape that turned my sorry-ass coochi snorcher into a kind of heaven.

"What does a vagina smell like?"

Earth.

Wet garbage.

God.

Water.

A brand-new morning.

Depth.

Sweet ginger.

Sweat.

Depends.

Musk.

Me.

No smell, I've been told.

Pineapple.

Chalice essence.

Paloma Picasso.

Earthy meat and musk.

Cinnamon and cloves.

Roses.

Spicy musky jasmine forest, deep, deep
forest.

Damp moss.

Yummy candy.

The South Pacific.

Somewhere between fish and lilacs.

Peaches.

The woods.

Ripe fruit.

Strawberry-kiwi tea.

Fish.

Heaven.

Vinegar and water.

Light, sweet liquor.

Cheese.

Ocean.

Sexy.

A sponge.

The beginning.

I have been traveling with this piece all over Amer-
ica (and now, the world) for over three years. I am
threatening to create a vagina-friendly map of all the
vagina-friendly cities I have visited. There are many
now. There have been many surprises; Oklahoma City
surprised me. They were wild for vaginas in Oklahoma
City. Pittsburgh surprised me. They love vaginas in
Pittsburgh. I have already been there three times. Wher-
ever I go, women come up to me after the show to tell me

their stories, to make suggestions, to communicate their responses. This is my favorite part of traveling with the work. I get to hear the truly amazing stories. They are told so simply, so matter-of-factly. I am always reminded how extraordinary women's lives are, and how profound. And I am reminded how isolated women are, and how oppressed they often become in their isolation. How few people they have ever told of their suffering and confusion. How much shame there is surrounding all this. How crucial it is for women to tell their stories, to share them with other people, how our survival as women depends on this dialogue.

It was after performing the piece one night in New York City that I heard the story of a young Vietnamese woman who, when she was five years old—recently arrived in America, unable to speak English—fell on a fire hydrant while playing with her best friend, and cut her vagina. Unable to communicate what had occurred, she simply hid her bloodied underpants under her bed. Her mother found them and assumed she'd been raped. As the young girl did not know the word for "fire hydrant," she could not explain to her parents what had really hap-

pened. Her parents accused her best friend's brother of raping her. They rushed the young girl to the hospital, and a whole group of men stood around her bed, staring at her open, exposed vagina. Then, on the way home, she realized her father was no longer looking at her. In his eyes she had become a used, finished woman. He never really looked at her again.

Or the story of the stunning young woman in Oklahoma, who approached me after the show with her stepmother to tell me how she had been born without a vagina, and only realized it when she was fourteen. She was playing with her girlfriend. They compared their genitals and she realized hers were different, something was wrong. She went to the gynecologist with her father, the parent she was close to, and the doctor discovered that in fact she did not have a vagina or a uterus. Her father was heartbroken, trying to repress his tears and sadness so his daughter would not feel bad. On the way home from the doctor, in a noble attempt to comfort her, he said, "Don't worry, darlin'. This is all gonna be just fine. As a matter of fact, it's gonna be great. We're gonna get you the best homemade pussy in America. And when you meet your husband, he's gonna know we had it made specially for him." And they did get her a new pussy, and she was relaxed and happy and when she brought her father back two nights later, the love between them melted me.

Then there was the night in Pittsburgh when a woman filled with passion rushed up to tell me she had to speak to me as soon as possible. Her intensity convinced me, and I called her as soon as I got back to New York. She said she was a massage therapist and she had to talk to me about the texture of the vagina. The texture was crucial. I hadn't gotten the texture, she said. And she talked to me for an hour with such detail, with such sensuous clarity, that when she was finished, I had to lie down. During that conversation she also talked to me about the word "cunt." I had said something negative about it in my performance, and she said I didn't understand the word at all. She needed to help me reconceive it. She talked to me for a half-hour more about the word "cunt" and when she was finished, I was a convert. I wrote this for her.

R E C L A I M I N G C U N T

I call it cunt. I've reclaimed it, "cunt." I really like it. "Cunt." Listen to it. "Cunt." C C, Ca Ca. Cavern, cackle, clit, cute, come—closed c—closed inside, inside ca—then u—then cu—then curvy, inviting sharkskin u—uniform, under, up, urge, ugh, ugh, u—then n then cun—snug letters fitting perfectly together—n—nest, now, nexus, nice, nice, always depth, always round in uppercase, cun, cun—n a jagged wicked electrical pulse—

n [high-pitched noise] then soft n—warm n—cun, cun, then t—then sharp certain tangy t—texture, take, tent, tight, tantalizing, tensing, taste, tendrils, time, tactile, tell me, tell me "Cunt cunt," say it, tell me "Cunt." "Cunt."

I ASKED A SIX-YEAR-OLD GIRL:

"If your vagina got dressed, what would it wear?"

"Red high-tops and a Mets cap worn backwards."

"If it could speak, what would it say?"

"It would say words that begin with 'V' and 'T'—'turtle' and 'violin' are examples."

"What does your vagina remind you of?"

"A pretty dark peach. Or a diamond I found from a treasure and it's mine."

"What's special about your vagina?"

"Somewhere deep inside it I know it has a really really smart brain."

"What does your vagina smell like?"

"Snowflakes."

THE WOMAN WHO LOVED TO MAKE VAGINAS HAPPY

I love vaginas. I love women. I do not see them as separate things. Women pay me to dominate them, to excite them, to make them come. I did not start out like this. No, to the contrary: I started out as a lawyer. But in my late thirties, I became obsessed with making women happy. There were so many unfulfilled women. So many women who had no access to their sexual happiness. It began as a mission of sorts, but then I got involved in it. I got very good at it, kind of brilliant. It was my art. I started getting paid for it. It was as if I had found my calling. Tax law seemed completely boring and insignificant then.

I wore outrageous outfits when I dominated women—lace and silk and leather—and I used props: whips, handcuffs, rope, dildos. There was nothing like this in tax law. There were no props, no excitement, and I hated those blue corporate suits, although I wear them now from time to time in my new line of work and they serve quite nicely. Context is all. There were no props, no outfits in corporate law. There was no wetness. There was no dark mysterious foreplay. There were no erect nipples. There were no delicious mouths, but mainly there was no moaning. Not the kind I'm talking about, anyway. This was the key, I see now; moaning was the thing that ultimately seduced me and got me addicted to making women happy. When I was a little girl and I would see women in the movies making love, making strange orgasmic moaning noises, I used to laugh. I got strangely hysterical. I couldn't believe that big, outrageous, ungoverned sounds like that just came out of women.

I longed to moan. I practiced in front of my mirror, on a tape recorder, moaning in various keys, various tones, with sometimes very operatic expressions, sometimes with more reserved, almost withheld expression. But always when I played it back, it sounded fake. It *was* fake. It wasn't rooted in anything sexual, really, only in my desire to be sexual.

But then when I was ten I had to pee really badly once. On a car trip. It went on for almost an hour and when I finally got to pee in this dirty little gas station, it was so exciting, I moaned. I moaned as I peed. I couldn't believe it, me moaning in a Texaco station somewhere in the middle of Louisiana. I realized right then that moans are connected with not getting what you want right away, with putting things off. I realized moans were best when they caught you by surprise; they came out of this hidden mysterious part of you that was speaking its own language. I realized that moans were, in fact, that language.

I became a moaner. It made most men anxious. Frankly, it terrified them. I was loud and they couldn't concentrate on what they were doing. They'd lose focus. Then they'd lose everything. We couldn't make love in people's homes. The walls were too thin. I got a reputation in my building, and people stared at me with contempt in the elevator. Men thought I was too intense; some called me insane.

I began to feel bad about moaning. I got quiet and polite. I made noise into a pillow. I learned to choke my moan, hold it back like a sneeze. I began to get headaches and stress-related disorders. I was becoming hopeless when I discovered women. I discovered that most women loved my moaning—but, more important, I discovered how deeply excited I got when other women moaned, when I could make other women moan. It became a kind of passion.

Discovering the key, unlocking the vagina's mouth, unlocking this voice, this wild song.

I made love to quiet women and I found this place inside them and they shocked themselves in their moaning. I made love to moaners and they found a deeper, more penetrating moan. I became obsessed. I longed to make women moan, to be in charge, like a conductor, maybe, or a bandleader.

It was a kind of surgery, a kind of delicate science, finding the tempo, the exact location or home of the moan. That's what I called it.

Sometimes I found it over a woman's jeans. Sometimes I sneaked up on it, off the record, quietly disarming the surrounding alarms and moving in. Sometimes I used force, but not violent, oppressing force, more like dominating, "I'm going to take you someplace; don't worry, lie back, enjoy the ride" kind of force. Sometimes it was simply mundane. I found the moan before things even started, while we were eating salad or chicken just casually right there, with my fingers, "Here it is like that," real simple, in the kitchen, all mixed in with the balsamic vinegar. Sometimes I used props—I loved props—sometimes I made the woman find her own moan in front of me. I waited, stuck it out until she opened herself. I wasn't fooled by the minor, more obvious moans. No, I pushed her further, all the way into her power moan.

There's the clit moan (a soft, in-the-mouth sound), the vaginal moan (a deep, in-the-throat sound), the combo clit-vaginal moan. There's the pre-moan (a hint of sound), the almost moan (a circling sound), the right-on-it moan (a deeper, definite sound), the elegant moan (a sophisticated laughing sound), the Grace Slick moan (a rock-singing sound), the WASP moan (no sound), the semireligious moan (a Muslim chanting sound), the mountaintop moan (a yodeling sound), the baby moan (a googie-googie-googie-goo sound), the doggy moan (a panting sound), the birthday moan (a wild-party sound), the uninhibited militant bisexual moan (a deep, aggressive, pounding sound), the machine-gun moan, the tortured Zen moan (a twisted, hungry sound), the diva moan (a high, operatic note), the twisted-toe-orgasm moan, and, finally, the surprise triple orgasm moan.

After I finished this piece I read it to the woman on whose interview I'd based it. She didn't feel it really had anything to do with her. She loved the piece, mind you, but she didn't see herself in it. She felt that I had some-how avoided talking about vaginas, that I was still some-how objectifying them. Even the moans were a way of objectifying the vagina, cutting it off from the rest of the

vagina, the rest of the woman. There was a real differ-ence in the way lesbians saw vaginas. I hadn't yet cap-tured it.

> *So I interviewed her again.*

"As a lesbian," she said, "I need you to start from a lesbian-centered place, not framed within a heterosexual context. I did not desire women, for example, because I disliked men. Men weren't even part of the equation." She said, "You need to talk about entering into vaginas. You can't talk about lesbian sex without doing this.

"For example," she said. "I'm having sex with a woman. She's inside me. I'm inside me. Fucking myself *together with her. There are four fingers inside me; two are hers, two are mine."*

I don't know that I wanted to talk about sex. But then again, how can I talk about vaginas without talking about them in action? I am worried about the titillation factor, worried about the piece becoming exploitative. Am I talking about vaginas to arouse people? Is that a bad thing?

"As lesbians," she said, "we know about vaginas. We touch them. We lick them. We play with them. We tease them. We notice when the clitoris swells. We notice our own."

I realize I am embarrassed, listening to her. There is a combination of reasons: excitement, fear, her love of vaginas and comfort with them and my distancing, terror of saying all this in front of you, the audience.

"I like to play with the rim of the vagina," she said, "with fingers, knuckles, toes, tongue. I like to enter it slowly, slowly entering, then thrusting three fingers inside.

"There's other cavities, other openings; there's the

mouth. While I have a free hand, there's fingers in her
mouth, fingers in her vagina, both going, all going all at
once, her mouth sucking my fingers, her vagina sucking
my fingers. Both sucking, both wet."

I realize I don't know what is appropriate. I
don't even know what that word means. Who de-
cides. I learn so much from what she's telling me.
About her, about me.

"Then I come to my own wetness," she says. "She
can enter me. I can experience my own wetness, let her
slide her fingers into me, her fingers into my mouth, my
vagina, the same. I pull her hand out of my cunt. I rub
my wetness against her knee so she knows. I slide my wet-
ness down her leg until my face is between her thighs."

Does talking about vaginas ruin the mystery,
or is that just another myth that keeps vaginas in
the dark, keeps them unknowing and unsatisfied?

"My tongue is on her clitoris. My tongue replaces
my fingers. My mouth enters her vagina."

Saying these words feels naughty, dangerous,
too direct, too specific, wrong, intense, in charge,
alive.

"My tongue is on her clitoris. My tongue replaces my fingers. My mouth enters her vagina."

To love women, to love our vaginas, to know them and touch them and be familiar with who we are and what we need. To satisfy ourselves, to teach our lovers to satisfy us, to be present in our vaginas, to speak of them out loud, to speak of their hunger and pain and loneliness and humor, to make them visible so they cannot be ravaged in the dark without great consequence, so that our center, our point, our motor, our dream, is no longer detached, mutilated, numb, broken, invisible, or ashamed.

"You have to talk about entering vaginas," she said. "Come on," I say, "come in."

I had been performing this piece for over two years when it suddenly occurred to me that there were no pieces about birth. It was a bizarre omission. Although when I told a journalist this recently, he asked me, "What's the connection?"

Almost twenty-one years ago I adopted a son, Dylan, who was very close in age to me. Last year he and his wife, Shiva, had a baby. They asked me to be present

for the birth. I don't think, in all my investigation, that I really understood vaginas until this moment. If I was in awe of them before the birth of my granddaughter, Colette, I am certainly in deep worship now.

I WAS THERE IN THE ROOM

For Shiva

I was there when her vagina opened.
We were all there: her mother, her husband,
    and I,
and the nurse from the Ukraine with her
    whole hand
up there in her vagina feeling and turning with
    her rubber
glove as she talked casually to us—like she was
    turning on a loaded faucet.

I was there in the room when the contractions
made her crawl on all fours,
made unfamiliar moans leak out of her pores
and still there after hours when she just
    screamed suddenly
wild, her arms striking at the electric air.

I was there when her vagina changed
from a shy sexual hole
to an archaeological tunnel, a sacred vessel,
a Venetian canal, a deep well with a tiny stuck
    child inside,
waiting to be rescued.

I saw the colors of her vagina. They changed.
Saw the bruised broken blue
the blistering tomato red
the gray pink, the dark;
saw the blood like perspiration along the edges
saw the yellow, white liquid, the shit, the clots
pushing out all the holes, pushing harder and
    harder,

saw through the hole, the baby's head

scratches of black hair, saw it just there behind

the bone—a hard round memory,

as the nurse from the Ukraine kept turning and
    turning

her slippery hand.

I was there when each of us, her mother and I,

held a leg and spread her wide pushing

with all our strength against her pushing

and her husband sternly counting, "One, two,
    three,"

telling her to focus, harder.

We looked into her then.

We couldn't get our eyes out of that place.

We forget the vagina, all of us

what else would explain

our lack of awe, our lack of wonder.

I was there when the doctor

reached in with Alice in Wonderland spoons

and there as her vagina became a wide operatic
     mouth
singing with all its strength;
first the little head, then the gray flopping arm,
     then the fast
swimming body, swimming quickly into our
     weeping arms.

I was there later when I just turned and faced
     her vagina.
I stood and let myself see
her all spread, completely exposed
mutilated, swollen, and torn,
bleeding all over the doctor's hands
who was calmly sewing her there.

I stood, and as I stared, her vagina suddenly
became a wide red pulsing heart.

The heart is capable of sacrifice.
So is the vagina.
The heart is able to forgive and repair.

It can change its shape to let us in.

It can expand to let us out.

So can the vagina.

It can ache for us and stretch for us, die for us

and bleed and bleed us into this difficult,

    wondrous world.

So can the vagina.

I was there in the room.

I remember.

ACKNOWLEDGMENTS

There are so many incredible people who helped give birth to this piece and then sustain it in the world. I want to thank the brave ones who brought it and me to their hometowns and colleges and theaters: Pat Cramer, Sarah Raskin, Gerald Blaise Labida, Howie Baggadonutz, Carole Isenberg, Catherine Gammon, Lynne Hardin, Suzanne Paddock, Robin Hirsh, Gali Gold.

A special thank-you to Steve Tiller and Clive Flowers for a gorgeous British premiere, and to Rada Boric for getting it done with style in Zagreb and for being my sister. Blessings on the generous, powerful women from the Center for Women War Victims in Zagreb.

I want to thank the extraordinary people at HERE Theatre in New York, who were crucial to the successful run of the play there: Randy Rollison and Barbara Busackino for their profound devotion and trust in this work; Wendy Evans Joseph for her magnificent set and great generosity; David Kelly; Heather Carson for her sexy, bold lights; Alex Avans and Kim Kefgen for their patience and perfection and for dancing the coochi snorcher dance with me night after night.

I want to thank Stephen Pevner for his great support in getting all this off the ground, and Robert Levithan for his trust. Thanks to Michele Steckler for being there again and again; Don Summa for getting the press to say the word; and

Alisa Solomon, Alexis Greene, Rebecca Mead, Chris Smith, Wendy Weiner, *Ms.*, *The Village Voice*, and *Mirabella* for talking about the piece with such love and respect.

I want to thank Gloria Steinem for her beautiful words and for being there before me, and Betty Dodson for loving vaginas and starting all this.

I want to thank Charlotte Sheedy for respecting me and fighting for me, and Marc Klein for his day-to-day work and his enormous support and patience. I want to thank Carol Bodie: her belief in me has sustained me through the lean years, and her advocacy has pushed the work past other people's fears and made it happen.

I want to thank Willa Shalit for her great faith in me, and for her talent and courage in bringing my work into the world. I want to thank David Phillips for being my ever-arriving angel, and Lauren Lloyd for the big gift of Bosnia. Thanks to Nancy Rose for her expert and kind guidance; a special thank-you to Marianne Schnall, Sally Fisher, Feminist.Com, and the V-Day Committee.

I want to thank Gary Sunshine for coming at the right time.

I want to thank my extraordinary editor, Mollie Doyle, for standing up for this book in more houses than one, and for ultimately being my great partner. I want to thank Marysue Rucci for seizing the project and helping me find its way as a book. I want to thank Villard for not being afraid.

Then there are my friends-blessings: Paula Allen, for jumping; Brenda Currin for changing my karma; Diana de Vegh, whose generosity healed me; James Lecesne, because he sees me and believes; Mark Matousek for forcing me deeper; Paula Mazur for taking the big journey; Thea Stone for staying with me; Sapphire, for pushing my boundaries; Kim Rosen, who lets me breathe and die.

I want to thank great women: Michele

McHugh, Debbie Schechter, Maxi Cohen, Judy Katz, Judy Corcoran, Joan Stein, Kathy Najimy, Teri Schwartz, and the Betty girls for constant love and support. I want to thank my mentors— Joanne Woodward, Shirley Knight, Lynn Austin, and Tina Turner.

I want to thank my mother, Chris; my sister, Laura; and my brother, Curtis, for finding the tangly way back to each other.

I want to acknowledge the brave, courageous women in the SWP program who keep facing the darkness over and over and riding through, particularly Maritza, Tarusa, Stacey, Ilysa, Belinda, Denise, Stephanie, Edwing, Joanne, Beverly, and Tawana.

I want to deeply acknowledge the hundreds of women who let me into their private places, who trusted me with their stories and secrets. May their stories lay the path for a free and safe world for Hannah, Katie, Molly, Adisa, Lulu, Allyson, Olivia, Sammy, Isabella, and others.

I want to thank my son, Dylan, for teaching me love, my daughter-in-law, Shiva, and my granddaughter, Coco, for birth.

Finally, I want to thank my partner, Ariel Orr Jordan, who co-conceived this piece with me, whose kindness and tenderness were a salve, were the beginning.

ABOUT THE AUTHOR

EVE ENSLER is a playwright and screenwriter. Her play *The Vagina Monologues* won a 1997 Obie Award and was nominated for a Drama Desk Award. It had a hit run Off-Broadway and has been touring throughout the country and internationally, including performances in Jerusalem, Zagreb, and London. Her play *Necessary Targets,* commissioned by the Joseph Papp Public Theater, was given a performance on Broadway to benefit Bosnian women refugees, and starred Meryl Streep and Angelica Huston. Her other plays include *Floating Rhoda and the Glue Man; Extraordinary Measures; The Depot; Scooncat; Loud in My Head; Lemonade; Ladies; Reef and Particle;* and *Cinderella Cendrillon.* Her articles have appeared in *Common Boundary, Ms.,* and the *Utne Reader.* She is currently working with Glenn Close on a screenplay about women in prison.